GETTING TO KNOW
THE WORLD'S
GREATEST COMPOSERS

G E O R G E
HANDEL

WRITTEN AND ILLUSTRATED BY MIKE VENEZIA

CONSULTANT

DONALD FREUND, PROFESSOR OF COMPOSITION, INDIANA UNIVERSITY SCHOOL OF MUSIC

CHILDRENS PRESS®
CHICAGO

Picture Acknowledgments
Music on cover and title page, Stock Montage, Inc.; 3, Anonymous,
Portrait of Friedrich Handel. Accademia Rossini, Bologna, Italy,
Giraudon/Art Resource, NY; 4 (left), The Newberry Library; 4
(right), Oliviero, Domenico. Interior of Teatro Regio. Museo
Civico, Turin, Italy. Scala/Art Resource, NY; 5, The Mansell
Collection; 6, North Wind Picture Archives; 7, Stock Montage,
Inc.; 12, North Wind; 15, Bibliothéque Nationale de France; 18-
19, Canaletto. Lo sposalizio del mare, Museo Pushkin, Moscow.
Scala/Art Resource, NY; 21, Stock Montage, Inc.; 24, The Bettmann Archive;
25, North Wind; 26-27, Canaletto, View of London from the
Thames. National Gallery, Prague, Czech Republic. Giraudon/Art
Resource, NY; 32, Stock Montage, Inc.

Project Editor: Shari Joffe
Design: PCI Design Group, San Antonio, Texas
Photo Research: Jan Izzo

Library of Congress Cataloging–in–Publication Data

Venezia, Mike.
    George Handel / written and illustrated by Mike Venezia.
    p.   cm. -- (Getting to know the world's greatest composers)
    ISBN 0-516-04539-3
    1. Handel, George Frideric, 1685-1759--Juvenile literature.
    2. Composers--Biography--Juvenile literature.
    [1. Handel, George Frideric, 1685-1759. 2. Composers.] I. Title.
    II. Series: Venezia, Mike. Getting to know the world's greatest composers.
    ML3930.H25V46 1995
    780' .92--dc20
    [B]   94-36345
                               CIP
                               AC MN

A portrait of
George Frideric Handel

George Frideric Handel was one of the
most famous composers in Europe during
the 1700s. He traveled all over Germany
and Italy, learning as much as he could about
the music of the day. In 1712, George Handel
moved to London, England. There he spent
the rest of his life composing some of the
greatest music ever written.

A concert of sacred music in a German cathedral in the 1700s

An Italian opera theater in the 1700s

In Germany, George Handel learned about choir music and organ music, which were played in the many churches there. In Italy, where opera was invented, he learned how songs could be performed beautifully by a single great singing star. He also learned how orchestra music was composed.

In 1749, to celebrate the signing of an important English peace treaty, Handel composed music for a special fireworks display in Green Park, London.

In England, George learned about important-sounding royal music, which was used to celebrate an event or honor a king or queen. George Handel often combined the different musical styles he had studied, and included them in his most famous musical pieces.

The house in Halle where George Handel was born

George Frideric Handel was born in the German town of Halle in 1685. Halle was a lively town while George was growing up. It had lots of places where he could hear music. Organ recitals and choir music were performed at the town's many churches. Town musicians played brass

German street
musicians of
the 1700s

instruments for special occasions,
and Halle had lots of street musicians,
too. George Frideric Handel also got
to meet many interesting people when
he was little. People from all over the
world came to see his father, who was
a well-known barber-surgeon.

As unusual as it seems today, during the 1600s and 1700s, barbers not only cut hair, but also were trained as doctors and operated on people!

George loved music from the time when he was very young. Unfortunately, his father didn't care for it at all. Mr. Handel thought

music was a waste of time, and that musicians
could never make a good living. He didn't
want George to study music or ever play an
instrument. There is a story that tells how
George's mother and aunt helped smuggle a
harpsichord into the attic so George could
practice quietly at night.

Whether the harpsichord story is true or not, George somehow learned to play music all by himself. When he was ten years old, his father took him along on a trip to the palace of the Duke of Weissenfels. While Mr. Handel went about his business, George found an organ in the duke's chapel and began to play it. The duke happened to be passing by and could hardly believe his ears. He had never heard such beautiful music being played by such a young boy.

The duke tried to convince Mr. Handel that his talented son deserved a chance to study music. As soon as he got back home, George began taking music lessons.

An old engraving of the German city of Hamburg

George learned quickly from his teacher, Friedrich Zachow, who was one of the best organists in Germany. George became an expert organ and harpsichord player, and began composing music. He also learned to play the violin and oboe.

George loved music so much that he decided to make it his career. When he was seventeen years old, he began traveling to other German cities that were known as important music centers. His first stop was Hamburg, where he got a job as a violinist and harpsichord player with the city's opera orchestra.

Operas were the top entertainment in Europe during Handel's time. They were as popular as movies are today. People loved to spend evenings listening to the great singers and watching them act out a story with beautiful costumes and scenery.

A sketch of the machinery built for
an opera stage set of the 1700s

A sketch showing how the same stage set would
look during the actual opera performance

They couldn't wait to find out what
special effects the stage designers
would come up with next. Sometimes
the designers built machines that were
able to show volcanos, or shipwrecks,
or strange, supernatural scenes.

While he was in Hamburg, George
met a talented singer and composer
named Johann Matteson.

Johann and George became best of friends, and helped each other with their music. Once, however, they had a serious argument and got into a duel with swords! The argument started when both of them wanted to play the harpsichord during an opera that Johann had written.

George Handel could be very stubborn,
especially when it came to music. Fortunately,
no one was seriously hurt during the fight,
and George and Johann soon became friends
again. In fact, Johann helped George write
his first opera. It was called *Almira*, and
became a big hit right away.

Lo sposalizio del mare, a view of Venice by 18th-century Italian artist Canaletto

George was happy about his success, but decided to leave Germany and go to Italy to learn more about operas. Italian operas were the most popular type in Europe. Italy had more opera houses and great singers than anywhere else in the world. While living there, George met—and studied the music of—such famous composers as Alessandro Scarlatti and Arcangelo Corelli. In Venice, Italy, George composed his first Italian opera. It became a big hit, too.

George Frideric Handel started to become famous all over Europe. In 1710, the ruler of the German state of Hanover, Georg Ludwig, heard about Handel. He asked him to head up his royal music department. George accepted the job, but soon after asked to be excused so he could

travel to London, England, where he had been invited to write operas. During the 1700s, England was behind the rest of Europe when it came to opera. People there were anxious to see and hear Italian operas—like the ones George Frideric Handel was writing.

$\mathcal{D}$uring his first few years in England, George Handel wrote many successful operas. He was even able to start his own opera company. But then, something happened. Slowly, people began losing interest in operas. The English people were becoming tired of listening to Italian songs they couldn't understand and stories that were usually very complicated.

Many of the opera stars had become spoiled, and demanded huge amounts of money to sing. Sometimes they even got into fights right on the stage. George Handel started losing money, and had to close his company. He became discouraged, but didn't give up. Handel started composing a different kind of music that he hoped his audience would enjoy more.

A performance of one of George Handel's
oratorios at London's Westminster Abbey

George Handel began writing
oratorios. An oratorio is similar to an
opera, except that a chorus, instead of
one or two great singing stars, sings
most of the music. Also, oratorios don't
have acting, costumes, or scenery.

Usually, George Handel wrote his oratorios about exciting stories from the Bible. The songs were sung in English, so that everyone in London could understand what was going on.

People loved Handel's new music. One reason his oratorios became so popular was that Handel had a special talent for creating music that helps you picture a story in your mind. Part of a famous Handel oratorio called *Israel in Egypt* tells how Moses, with the help of God, sent millions of flies to irritate the Egyptian pharaoh. Moses did this to convince the pharoah to stop using the people of Israel as slaves.

Singers in Handel's oratorios in London

The high voices of the women chorus members and the quick rhythm of the violins used in the piece lets you almost see and feel pesty flies swarming all over the place!

Handel also composed music just for instruments. It's easy to picture the excitement and grandness of a royal boat party in his most famous orchestra work, *Water Music*. Handel wrote the *Water Music* for his old boss, Georg Ludwig of Germany, who had become George I, King of England, in 1714.

Handel wrote *Water Music* for a grand royal concert on London's Thames River in 1717. While King George I floated along on his royal barge, Handel conducted 50 musicians on a nearby boat!

George Frideric Handel's most famous piece is an oratorio called *Messiah*. It is about the life of Jesus Christ. The words that are sung to it come right out of the Bible. *Messiah* was first performed in Dublin, Ireland. It was written to help raise money for poor people, the same way many concert performances do today.

Handel felt deeply inspired when he wrote his most famous work. He used everything he had learned in the past. When you listen to the *Messiah*, you can hear a combination of Italian opera-style singing, English orchestral music, and German church music. The piece also includes many different moods, from very happy to very solemn.

So many people in Dublin were
anxious to hear *Messiah* that newspapers
there printed up ads asking women not
to wear their usual hooped skirts and
men not to wear swords. They wanted
to make sure there was room for everyone
in the music hall.

Even though *Messiah* was very successful in Ireland, it didn't go over very well back in London. Church leaders there didn't like the idea of having any kind of entertainment about the life of Jesus. They tried to convince people that *Messiah* was disrespectful, and that they shouldn't see it.

George decided it might be better to perform his

oratorio just once a year, for charity. George Frideric Handel was a very generous person. He donated lots of his time to raise money for poor people. His favorite charity was the foundling hospital. The foundling hospital took care of babies who had no parents. For many years, Handel performed his *Messiah* right at the hospital.

In April of 1759, after giving a performance of the *Messiah*, George Frideric Handel became ill. He died eight days later, at the age of seventy-four. Even though he composed many well-loved operas, oratorios, and orchestra pieces, the *Messiah* was his favorite. Eventually, the *Messiah* became appreciated in London. Today, it is considered one of the world's great music masterpieces.

It's pretty easy to find Handel's music on the radio or on tapes and compact discs at your local library. At Christmastime, some cities put on special performances of the *Messiah* in which the public is invited to join the chorus.

ause...

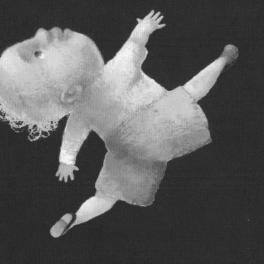

VLADIMIR RADUNSKY

New York London Toronto Sydney

This is me. I live over there in that red house.
Actually, other people live there too.
Here's my friend Maria: She only seems tall because she never
takes off her skates.
And over there are Mr. and Mrs. Qurlesbarles. Mr. Q. can hold
a cane on one finger, just like a clown in the circus!
Mrs. Q. doesn't like it when he does that.
We also have lots of dogs and cats: hundreds, maybe
even thousands.

All of my friends go out to play with their mothers, their
baby-sitters, their fathers, even their dogs.
But me . . . I have Grandma. Everybody calls her Mrs. Duncan.

Here she is! I love my grandma, really, but she just always
embarrasses me.
Every minute, every hour, every day of the week!

Monday

Grandma and I go for a walk.

Mr. and Mrs. Q. are already outside.

It's so early and quiet, Mr. Q. hasn't even started doing his tricks with the cane.

All of a sudden... Grandma leapfrogs over Mrs. Q.!

Mrs. Q. is very cross, but Mr. Q. just giggles.

Mrs. Duncan, why did you do that, dear?

BECause...

See what I mean?

Tuesday

Our old dog Pavlov is peacefully lying on his side in the middle of the lawn, staring nowhere special. Then he rolls over on his back and yawns. Then he yawns again and rolls over on his other side.

Wednesday

Grandma does something really goofy!

Maria is outside roller-skating. She's always roller-skating;

I've never even seen her walk!

Why are you SLidiNG after me, Mrs. Duncan?

Grandma squeals, drops my hand, and runs after Maria.
Maria freaks out!

It's so funny! Grandma is really skating without the skates!

BECause...

Wednesday night

'cause 'cause be-be-be

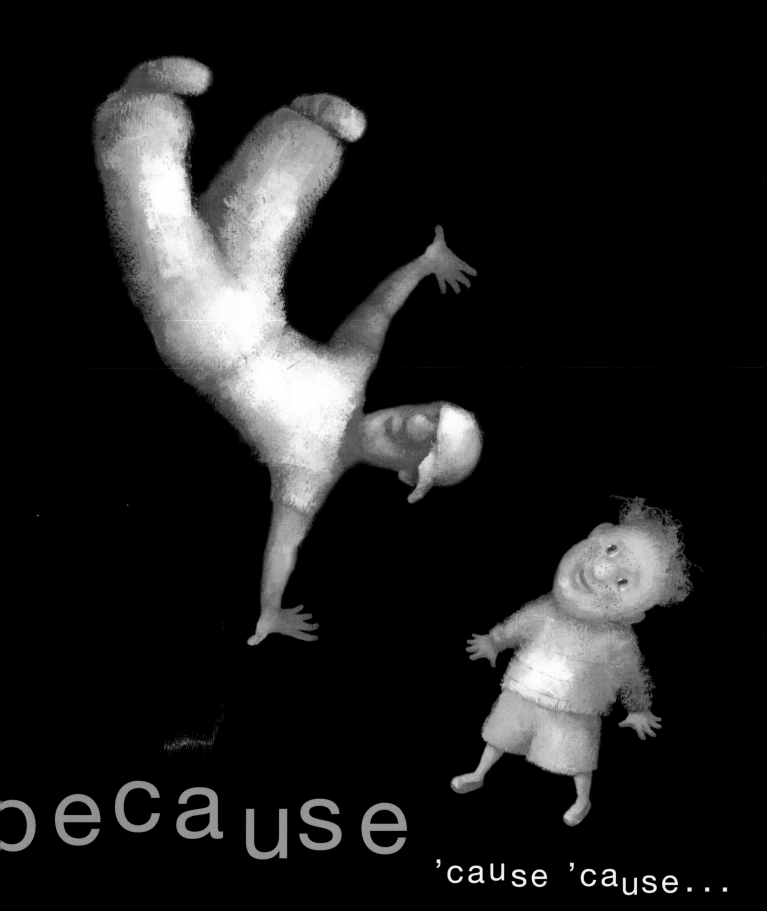

because

'cause 'cause...

Thursday morning

I had a cool dream.
First there was this huge bang, and Grandma was tap-dancing with Mr. Q.'s cane.
Then I saw Grandma doing cartwheels. She made my head spin!
I don't remember anything else. I woke up.
Wow, I'd like to move like that too!

Friday

Zzzzzz...That's our big fan. Grandma is crazy about it. Every time it's on, Grandma runs around it in circles and then flaps her arms like a butterfly.

Grandma,

why are you **flapping**

like a butterfly?

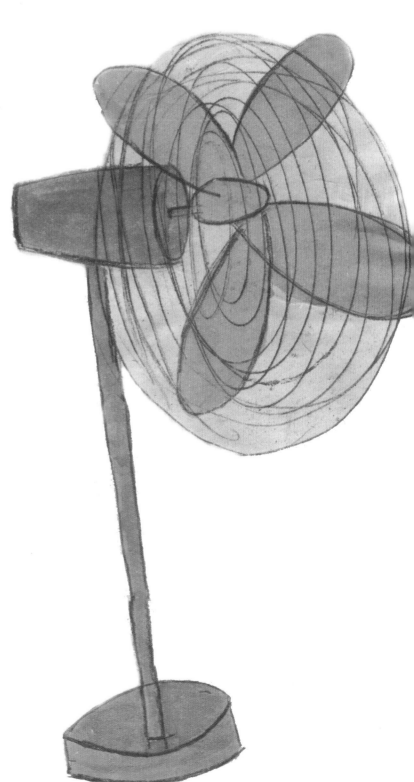

BECause...

Friday afternoon

Grandma loves meeting me after school.

She's the first one there and waits till we come out.

The crossing guard always makes us march across the street.

This is Grandma's chance to drive the guard really crazy.

Mrs. Duncan, why are we swinging? BECause...

Saturday

We're in the park. The park is great! There is always a ranger
with his horse there. I like the horse. Grandma likes the horse too.
Today Grandma whinnies happily and takes off in a gallop!
It's really fun! Everybody likes that, except the ranger
and his horse.

Neigh...
Mrs. Duncan,
why are you
galloping?

Neigh... neigh...

BECause...

Neigh... neigh...

Sunday

It's a beautiful day!

Everybody is outside wearing his best clothes.

Grandma is beaming!

Then all of a sudden she leaps up... and flies!

Higher and higher in the sky. Maria and I leap too!

So do some of our neighbors!

People are clapping like crazy and screaming their heads off!

Bravo!

Bravo!

Bravo!

Woof, woof, hurray!

Meow... Mrs. Duncan, why?

BECause... I—

am-a-dancer!

to E.R.

—V. R.

Atheneum Books for Young Readers - An imprint of Simon & Schuster Children's Publishing Division

1230 Avenue of the Americas - New York, New York 10020

Text copyright © 2007 by Mikhail Baryshnikov and Vladimir Radunsky - Illustrations copyright © 2007 by Vladimir Radunsky

Book design by Vladimir Radunsky. Prepress Katharina Gasterstadt.

The text for this book is set in Helvetica and Ingredients. The illustrations are rendered in gouache on paper.

Manufactured in China

First Edition

10   9   8   7   6   5   4   3   2   1

Library of Congress Cataloging-in-Publication Data

Baryshnikov, Mikhail, 1948–

Because . . . / Mikhail Baryshnikov ; illustrated by Vladimir Radunsky.

— 1st ed.

p.   cm.

"Ginee Seo books."

Summary: A young boy who lives with his grandmother is terribly embarrassed by her behavior at first, but comes to realize that she is not just having fun, she has a reason for each strange action.

ISBN-13: 978-0-689-87582-3

ISBN-10: 0-689-87582-7

[1. Eccentrics and eccentricities—Fiction. 2. Grandmothers—Fiction. 3. Dancers—Fiction.] I. Radunsky, Vladimir, ill. II. Title.

PZ7.B287Bec 2007

[E]—dc22

2006025728